The Snowman ™

CONCERT SUITE FOR STRING QUARTET

SCORE

Music by

Howard Blake

CHESTER MUSIC

part of *The Music Sales Group*

London / New York / Paris / Sydney / Copenhagen / Berlin / Madrid / Hong Kong / Tokyo

Duration: c. 11 minutes

Published by
CHESTER MUSIC LIMITED
14-15 Berners Street, London W1T 3LJ, UK.

Exclusive Distributors:
MUSIC SALES LIMITED
Distribution Centre, Newmarket Road, Bury St Edmunds, Suffolk IP33 3YB, UK.
MUSIC SALES CORPORATION
180 Madison Avenue, 24th Floor, New York NY 10016, USA.
MUSIC SALES PTY LIMITED
Units 3-4, 17 Willfox Street, Condell Park, NSW 2200, Australia.

Order No. CH80971
ISBN: 978-1-78305-003-1

Music by Howard Blake © 1982 by Highbridge Music Ltd.

The Snowman is recorded complete on Sony 71116.
The piano score of *The Snowman* is available separately: CH76879.
The sheet music of *Walking in the Air* is available separately: CH77110.

Printed in the EU.

The Snowman Concert Suite
(for string quartet)

HOWARD BLAKE
Opus 457 1993

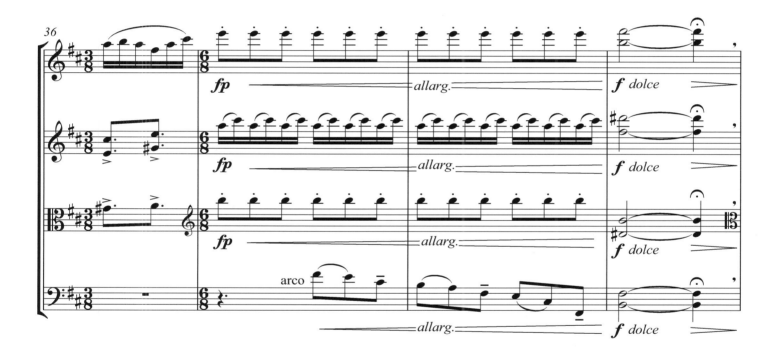

4

4 Moderato ♩ = 96

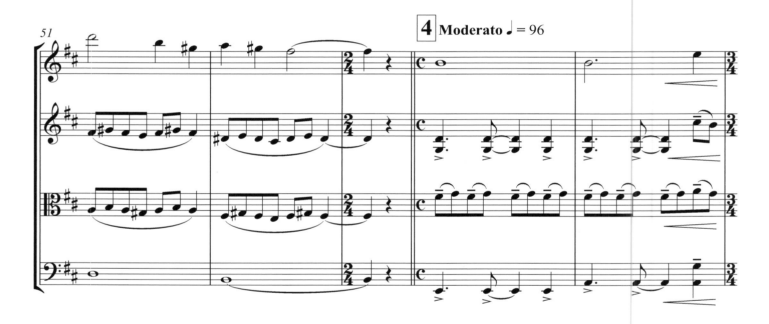

6

9 A Tempo

11

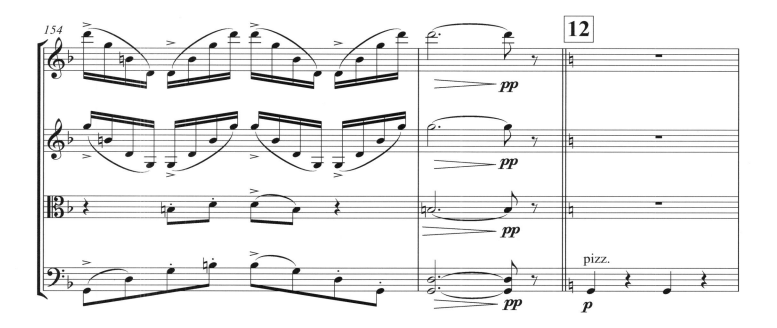

13 ♩. = 120

15

20

Tranquillo ♩ = 96 **17**

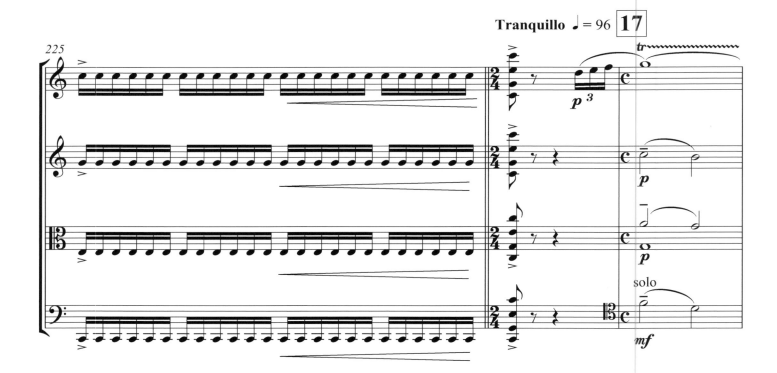

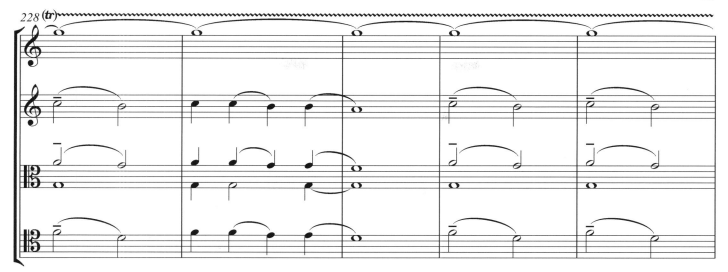

22

18   allargando

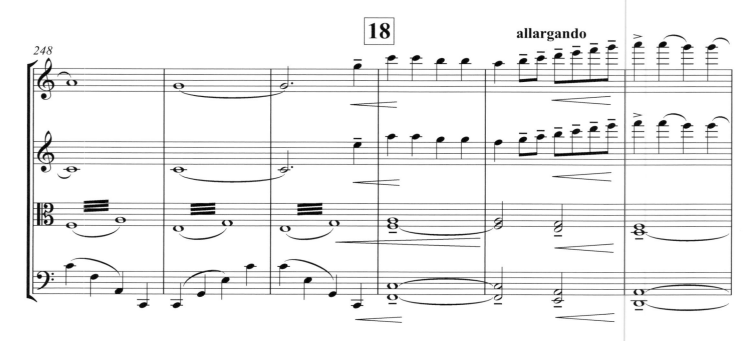

a tempo   poco rit.   8va

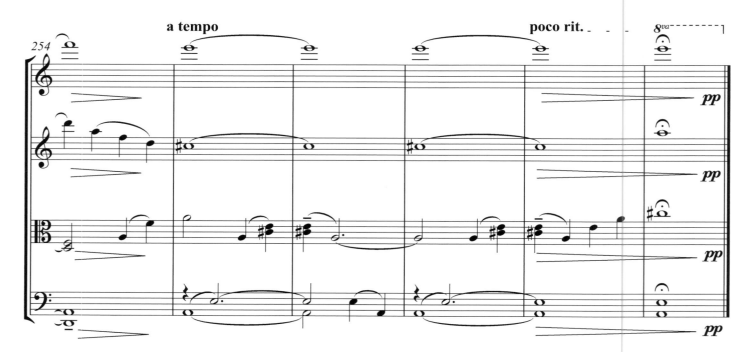

123456789

Other publications featuring The Snowman *include:*

THE SNOWMAN
Easy Piano Picture Book
BLAKE
CH76890

THE SNOWMAN
Piano Score
BLAKE
CH76879

THE SNOWMAN
Suite for Violin & Piano
BLAKE
CH76901

THE SNOWMAN
Suite for Easy Piano
BLAKE
CH76912

THE SNOWMAN
Suite for Flute & Piano
BLAKE
CH77066

THE SNOWMAN
Suite for Cello & Piano
BLAKE
CH77099

THE SNOWMAN
Full Score
BLAKE
CH77176

WALKING IN THE AIR
Flute & Piano
BLAKE
CH76923

WALKING IN THE AIR
Easy Piano
BLAKE
CH77055

WALKING IN THE AIR
Trumpet/Cornet & Piano
BLAKE
CH77077

WALKING IN THE AIR
Clarinet/Tenor Sax
& Piano
BLAKE
CH77088

WALKING IN THE AIR
Voice & Piano
BLAKE
CH77110

CHESTER MUSIC
part of *The Music Sales* Group
www.musicsalesclassical.com

CH80971
ISBN 978-1-78305-003-1
9 781783 050031

Michael Nyman

Four Ostinatos
for Solo Bass Clarinet

Chester Music